MAKING TOYS
That Move

Gillian Chapman
Pam Robson

SIMON & SCHUSTER
YOUNG BOOKS

To Rupert

The toys in this book are not suitable playthings for very young children.
Parents and teachers should satisfy themselves that children carrying out the projects are
mature enough to do so safely.

This book was prepared for
Simon & Schuster Young Books by
Globe Education of Nantwich, Cheshire

Visualisation and design: Gillian Chapman
Photography: Rupert Horrox

First published in 1994
by Simon & Schuster Young Books
Campus 400
Maylands Avenue
Hemel Hempstead, Herts HP2 7EZ

A catalogue record for this book is available
from the British Library

ISBN 0 7500 1531 4

Printed and bound in Hong Kong
by Wing King Tong Ltd

Contents

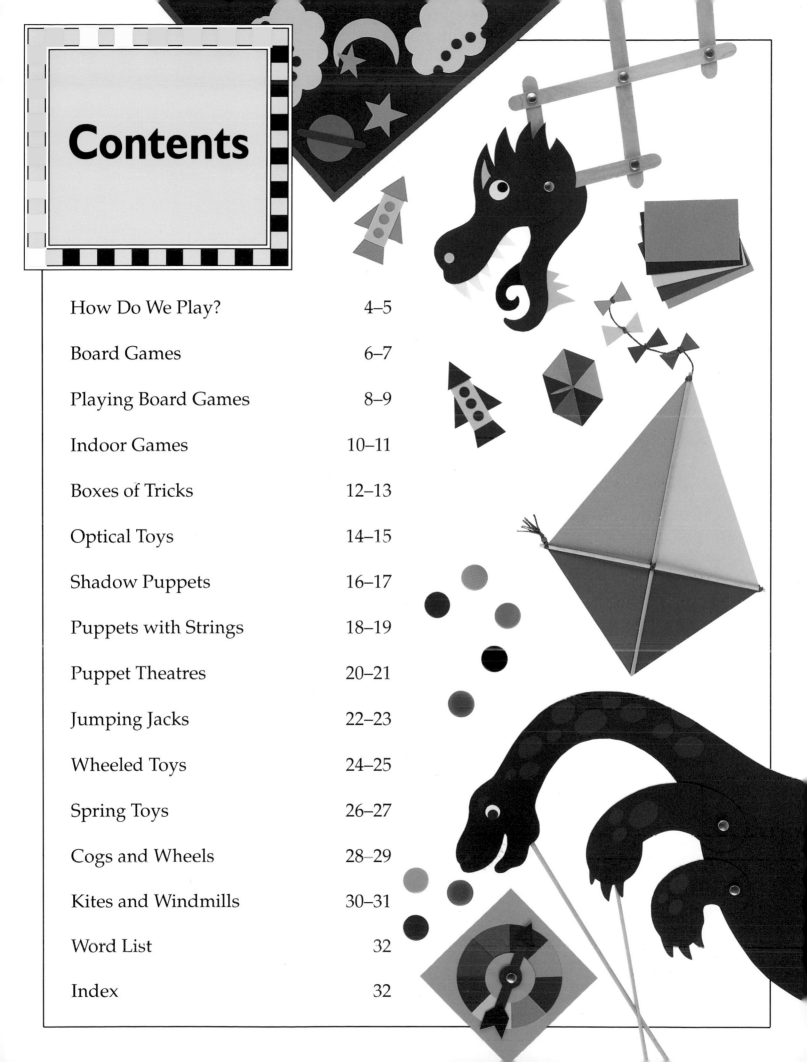

How Do We Play?

Young animals always play. By mimicking their parents they learn the rules of survival. Children's games usually reflect events in their day to day lives. Play can be a solitary or social activity. It can be competitive or co-operative. Many games require special strengths or skills—chess is a game of **strategy** where one player is battling against another. Some games involve an element of chance, where dice are thrown.

Moving Toys and Games

Since earliest times play has been important. The first toys and games satisfied a need in children to mimic grown-ups. Toys like hobby horses and dolls were popular with children in ancient Greece. Moving toys that copy human or animal behaviour have always had appeal, even to adults.

Toy Cat
Moveable jaw, bronze teeth and crystal eyes—Egypt, 1300 BC.

Toy Mouse
Moveable jaw and tail—Egypt, 1300 BC.

Puppets have entertained grown-ups and children for centuries. A wooden cat with jaws that move can be seen in the British Museum—it was made by the ancient Egyptians. Some of the earliest board games made out of clay or stone are also Egyptian. These natural materials are **durable**, so the games can still be seen today in museums.

Play is Fun

For centuries children have used toys and games to learn about life. Nineteenth century toys were learning tools rather than playthings. Nowadays, play is often both educational and fun!

Toy Horse
Painted wood with wheels—Egypt, 200 BC.

Toys illustrated on this page are reproduced by courtesy of the Trustees of the British Museum.

Materials for Playthings

Look at your toys and games and find out what materials they are made from. They are probably made from **synthetic materials** like plastic. Today, most playthings are mass produced in factories but there was a time when toys and games were all made by hand from natural materials found near the home. A piece of bark became a toy boat to float on water. A ball could be made from an animal bladder.

Toys from Junk!

In parts of southern Africa, toys are now made from junk materials. Children make intricately constructed wire models with moving wheels. Scrap metal, plastic and wood are used to make toy bicycles, lorries and aeroplanes. In 1985, a toy-making contest was sponsored by the museum in Mochudi, a village in Botswana. Today, the villagers make moving toys for sale.

Designing Toys and Games

To design a successful toy is not easy. Hand-held toys and games must feel comfortable to hold—they must have what we call a **tactile** quality. They must be safe to play with, have no sharp edges and contain no harmful substances. Above all, they must be durable—they need to last for a long time. In addition to these basic requirements, they should look good and be fun to play with.

Board Games

A board game, whether for one or many players, must be carefully designed. It is important to choose materials with the right properties for the board and accessories. The board must be **rigid** and durable, but not too heavy. The dice and counters should be the right size and shape to suit the game and be light and easy to handle. Consider all these qualities in your design. Also, think about how you will store the game when it is not in use.

Counters
Make the counters to suit the theme of the game. They must be easy to see on the board and each player must be able to recognise their own counter. The number of counters needed will depend on the number of players. Clean and decorate natural objects, like pebbles, shells or seeds. Make original counter shapes from stiff card or self-hardening clay, or use junk items like beads, buttons or plastic tops.

Dice
Dice are usually cube-shaped, but can take many shapes and forms. The Indian game of pachisi is played with cowrie shells as dice. Scoring depends on the number of shells landing mouth-uppermost. Paint a set of pebbles with dots or stripes, or make pyramid shapes marked at the **vertices** for scoring. A simple teetotum or twizzler can be made using the pattern below. It can have six or eight numbered sides.

Spinners
A spinner can be made from rigid card. Draw a large circle on the card, divide it into equal segments and put a score in each. Cut an arrow shape as long as the diameter of the circle out of stiff card. Mark the centre of the arrow and attach it with a paper fastener through the centre of the circle so that it swivels. You can stiffen the arrow and protect the spinner by covering them both with clear, adhesive film.

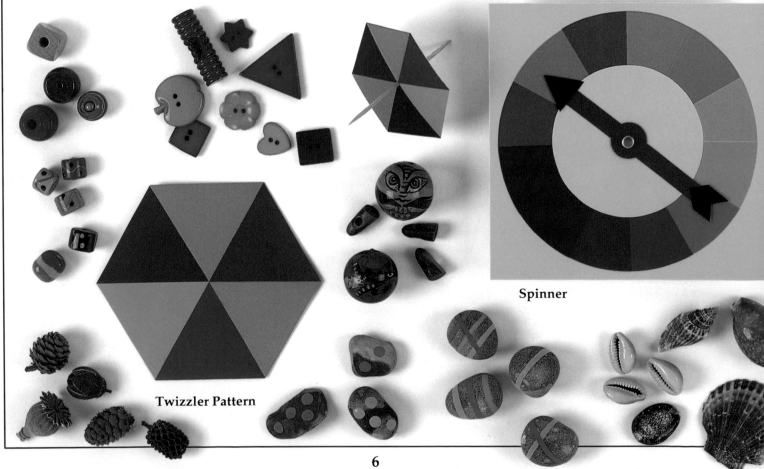

Twizzler Pattern

Spinner

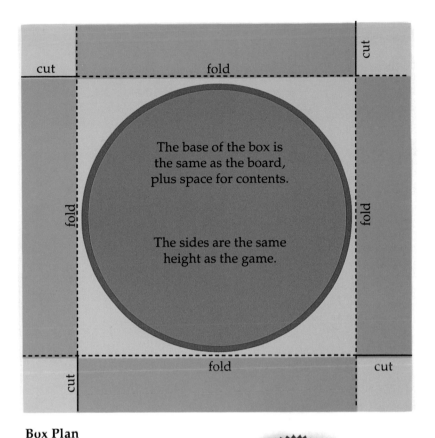

The base of the box is the same as the board, plus space for contents.

The sides are the same height as the game.

Box Plan

Storing Board Games

To make a box for your board game, measure a square of strong card as shown here. The board should fit within the scored lines. Cut and fold as directed to make the sides of the box. Join the sides by glueing or stapling. You have used your 2-D shape to build a strong, 3-D, protective structure.

The box lid can be made in the same way but needs to be slightly larger. Attach the rules for the game inside the lid and decorate the box inside and out. With the circular board use the empty spaces inside the box to hold the pieces. A good design takes into account both function and appearance.

Magnetic Maze Game

Here is a magnetic board game for one person to play. It works because **magnetic forces** travel through non-magnetic material. Design a really complicated maze on a circle of card. The card will need to be rigid but not thick enough to weaken the power of the magnet.

Make a character to guide through the maze (we have chosen an hedgehog). Use card or clay and push a steel drawing pin or paper-clip through the bottom. Hold a magnet underneath the board to guide the hedgehog through the maze. The magnet attracts the steel pin allowing you to move the hedgehog.

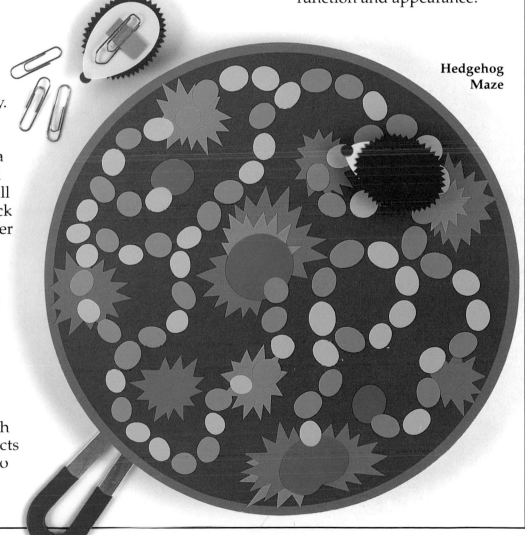

Hedgehog Maze

Playing Board Games

A competitive board game, like a racing game, involves a number of players. A challenge game, involving strategy in which an opponent must be defeated, often needs only two players. When designing a game begin by asking questions. How many players? Is the board rigid, durable and **portable**? Is it large enough? Which shape is best—round or **polygonal**? Will you need to fold it? What are the rules of the game?

A Folding Game Board
Measure the shape of the board on stiff card and cut it out in two separate halves. Position the boards as shown. Tape the two halves together, folding over the extra tape at each end. Turn the board over and tape along the gap on the other side. Reinforce the sides of the board with tape to strengthen and protect it.

Survival Challenge

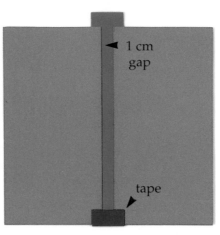

1 cm gap

tape

Tape edges for protection.

Making a Folding Game Board

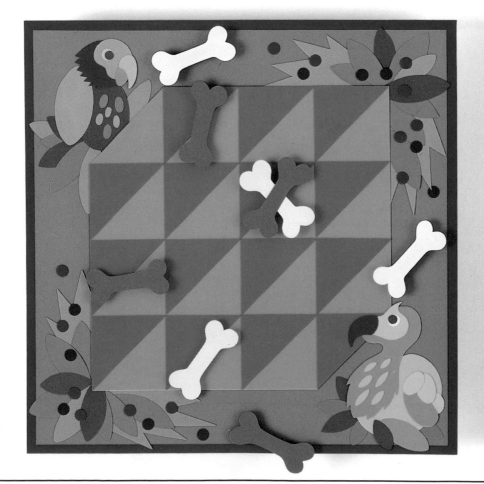

Draw the game on paper which is cut slightly smaller than the size of the board. Carefully score the paper along the centre fold, align with the fold on the inside of the board and glue firmly. You may decide to protect the board with clear, adhesive film. To complete the board, decorate the outside too.

A Challenge Game
Design a challenge game for two players in which the aim is to knock out your opponent. Think of an environmental theme. For example, which animal will survive extinction? The counters here are bones and the board folds along the **diagonal**. Can you design a box to contain and protect a triangular board?

A Race Game

The space race game shown here is a game for eight players. The aim is for each 'astronaut' to visit every planet in our solar system, then return to Earth. Because there are eight players a regular **octagon** shape has been chosen for the board. When the board is folded away it becomes an irregular **hexagon**. How could you reinforce or strengthen the vulnerable corners on this board? There are many aspects to designing a game that have to be considered. The most important is that the game should be fun to play.

Game Box

Space Race Game

Playing the Game

A special 'launch code sequence' must be scored by spinning the twizzler to decide who starts. The twizzler itself is octagonal to match the board. To make the game exciting obstacles are placed in the way of the players. These are described on hazard cards. There may be space debris, aliens or meteors to avoid, or perhaps fuel runs low. The counters are colour-coded rockets.

Designing the Box

The game box shown above contains the folded board. Separate partitions have been made in the box to hold all the game pieces. By cutting slits in lengths of card these sections can be slotted together without glueing.

9

Indoor Games

Dominoes is one of the most popular indoor games in the world and was possibly first played long ago in China. It was originally a game of chance. A modern European set has twenty-eight pieces, including one blank. The first sets were made from wood, ivory or bone. Dominoes, like most indoor games, are subjected to much handling during play so both their tactile quality and durability are important.

Picture Dominoes
To make a game of picture dominoes, first choose six different symbols. Arrange the symbols in pairs, including a blank, and use every combination. You should have 28 pairs. Measure and cut 28 identical cards. Glue the symbols to the cards and protect them with clear, adhesive film. To play, four players each have 7 dominoes. Take turns to play all your dominoes by matching up the symbols.

Picture Dominoes

Growing Families

Growing Families
To make this card game you will need to measure and cut identical pieces of stiff card to make the 'pack'. The game requires each player to collect sets of four cards to make 'family' groups. We have used tree families. Players aim to collect as many complete families as possible. This is another tactile game. Playing cards must be both rigid and light. They must also be strong and attractive.

The Bug Game

This can be a 2-D or 3-D game. You can either draw flat shapes out of stiff card, using the pattern shown here, and join them by lying them flat on a table, or you can make slits in some of the pieces so that they can be slotted together. In this way, as the game progresses, flat shapes turn into 3-D bugs.

To play the game you will need a twizzler or a die. The numbers from 1 to 6 match the bug part. Some parts of the bug, like the antennae, are very thin. How could they be strengthened? The first player to complete a bug wins!

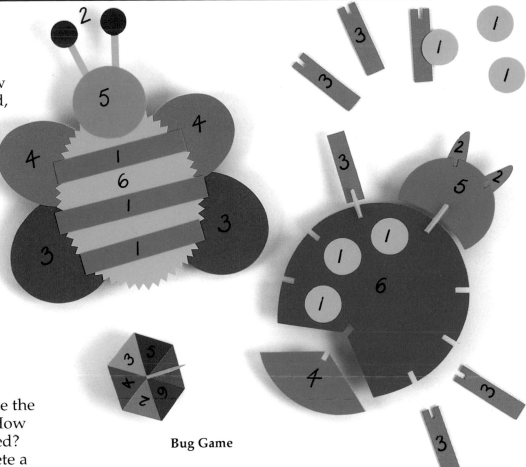

Bug Game

Anti-pollution Game

Anti-Pollution Game

Decorate a deep cardboard box with an underwater scene. Almost fill the box with crumpled up blue tissue paper. Make some 'rubbish' and 'fish' shapes from thin card. Attach a paper-clip hook to each and mark with a score. Hide them in the waves.

Make a fishing rod, attaching a length of string with an open paper-clip at one end. The aim of the game is to hook as much rubbish as possible out of the sea. The highest scores will be for removing rubbish, the lowest for catching fish.

Try this game using magnets instead of hooks. Can you fish for rubbish through real water using magnets?

Boxes of Tricks

The Chinese were the first to design elaborately decorated boxes to hold a variety of fascinating puzzles and tricks. Such games often require numerous tiny, but vital, pieces. You can construct a useful partitioned box to hold your tricks. The partitions can be slotted or glued in place. Make sure that you allow sufficient space for each trick, particularly if they are different shapes and sizes like the ones shown here.

Spillikins

The aim of the game is to spill the coloured sticks into a pile, then pick them up singly without moving any others. If the spillikin pile is on a shiny surface, they will move more easily, so the game is better played on a carpet. Use 50 wooden kebab sticks. They are light and can be coloured easily. Each colour has a score and the player with the highest score wins the game.

Spillikins

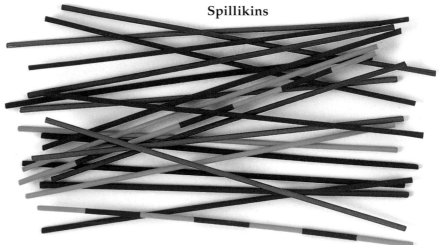

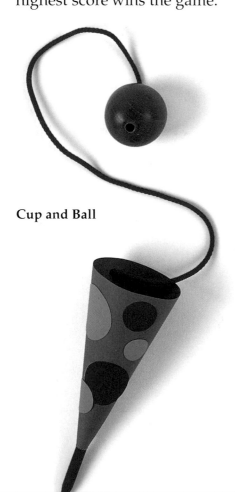

Cup and Ball

Cup and Ball

This simple catching game can be played in two ways. The bead can be caught either in the funnel or on the point of the stick. Make a funnel from strong, **flexible** card. Attach it to the blunt end of a short stick. Tie a length of strong thread to the funnel with a large bead on the free end. Flick the 'cup' and try to catch the 'ball'.

Matchstick Puzzles

Only make use of spent matches for these challenging puzzles. Can you arrange three matchsticks in a triangle without any of the 'heads' touching the surface beneath?

Change the triangle below into three connecting triangles using the same number of matches.

Matchstick Puzzles

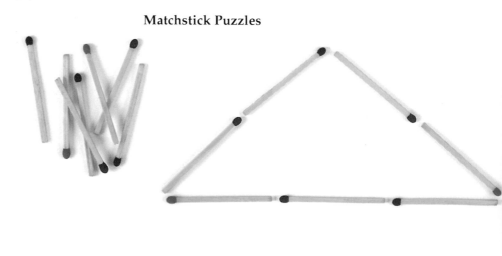

Tangrams

Use the pattern below to trace your seven pieces, or tans, and cut them out of stiff card. Laminating the pieces will make them last longer. How many designs can you make? There are 1,600 possible designs. All the pieces must be used each time and none must overlap.

Tangram Pattern

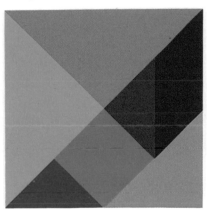

Box of Tricks

The Magic Square

Numbers have fascinated people since ancient times. In this magic square, every row—**vertical**, **horizontal** and diagonal—totals 15. Make the square from coloured card as shown here. Number nine plastic or card counters and ask your friend to position them correctly.

Picking 'Fruit'

The aim of this puzzle is to remove the 'fruit' from the 'branch'. It will only work if a strong, flexible fabric like felt is used. Cut three slits as shown and thread string through them. Attach a large bead to each end of the string. Now try to remove the string and beads.

Keeping Tidy

Every puzzle should fit neatly inside the box making best use of all the partitions. Secure together the numerous small pieces for each trick or puzzle so that no important parts are lost. Spillikins can be bound in a bundle and will fit into a long, narrow section of the box.

Release the beads by pushing the middle felt strip through the small slot.

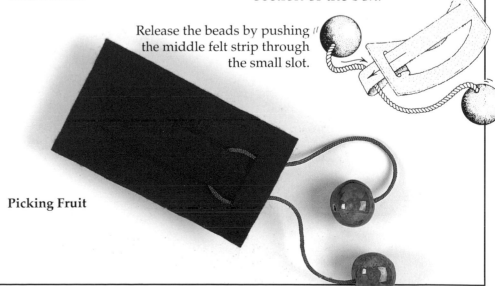

Magic Square

Picking Fruit

Optical Toys

Optical toys work because light travels in straight lines and is reflected from shiny surfaces. Reflections in flat mirrors are always reversed left to right because the light bounces off the mirror like a ball bouncing off the ground. When the light leaves the mirror some of it enters your eyes. Flat mirrors are used inside periscopes and kaleidoscopes. In a periscope, the second mirror corrects the reversed image.

Constructing a Kaleidoscope

You will need a strong card tube about 6 cm in diameter and 20 cm long. Using mirror board make an elongated, triangular, box shape that will fit inside the tube. The reflective surfaces of the mirror board should be on the inside of the box. To hold the triangle in place, pad the spaces left inside the tube with tissue paper.

Put a selection of small, coloured shapes into a Cellophane bag and tape it across one end of the tube. Cover the other end with dark paper and make a viewing hole in the centre. Cover the outside of the kaleidoscope with paper and decorate it.

Using the Kaleidoscope

To view the patterns inside the kaleidoscope, hold it towards the light while looking through the viewing hole. The coloured shapes are reflected from the mirrored sides of the triangular box so the pattern is repeated several times. Shake the kaleidoscope and the patterns change.

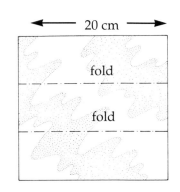

Kaleidoscope

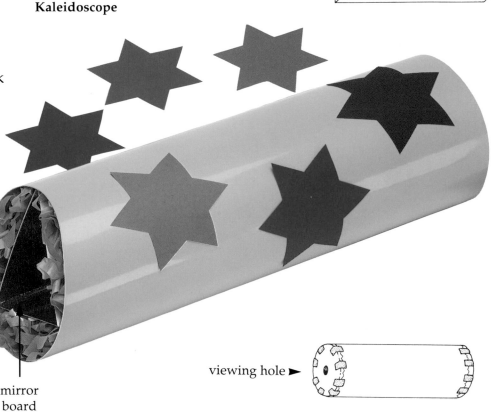

padding

mirror board

Put coloured shapes into a Cellophane bag.

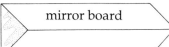

viewing hole ►

Constructing a Periscope

Using the plan below make a long box from strong card. Make two triangular supports as shown. These ensure that both mirrors are parallel to each other and at an angle of 45° to the sides of the box. Attach the mirrors to the supports. Fix the **structures** one at either end of the box so that the mirrors face each other. Secure them in place with tape across the top and bottom of the periscope. Decorate the outside of the box—camouflage colours might be appropriate. Now the periscope is ready to use.

Using the Periscope

The periscope makes it possible to see around corners or over the top of high obstacles. One mirror receives light coming from the object viewed and reflects it to the second mirror which in turn reflects it into the eyes of the viewer.

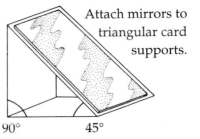

Attach mirrors to triangular card supports.

90°   45°

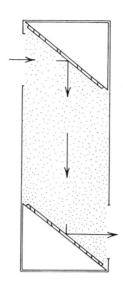

Position of Mirrors ▲
How light travels through a periscope.

Periscope ►

Periscope Plan ▼

window

window

To make the periscope fold along the lines and glue down the end flap.

Shadow Puppets

Shadow is the absence of light. If you want to make puppets that create totally black shadows you will need rigid, **opaque** card that light cannot pass through. To make puppets that will cast shadows in colour use stiff coloured paper that allows some light through. Another way is to make coloured card **translucent** by soaking it in liquid paraffin but this must be done by an adult.

Light and Shadow

When light is obstructed by an opaque material, it bounces back towards the light source creating a shadow. The light source for a shadow puppet theatre must always be positioned behind the puppet. The screen is in front. The closer the light source is to the puppet, the larger the shadow. A small light source will create a sharp, black shadow, a bigger one will cause fuzziness around the edges of the shadow. The puppeteer must keep away from the path of the light to prevent unwanted shadows.

Cat and Mice Shadow Puppets

Simple Shadow Puppets

A shadow puppet is a two-dimensional shape. For this reason a static character is always drawn and cut in profile. Before you design the characters, think about which direction they will be facing on the screen. Try to have both left and right handed figures. If two characters are holding a conversation they must be facing each other. First try simple shapes like the mice shown here.

The rods that work the puppets can be positioned horizontally or vertically depending on where you want to stand—either in the 'wings' or below the screen. How are you going to attach the rods? Try using drawing pins, tape or Velcro.

split pin ▲ joint

Attach rods with ▶ tape, velcro or drawing pins.

Jointed Shadow Puppets
Your puppets must be made in proportion to the size of the theatre screen and the sticks you use must be strong enough to support them. Only two rods can be fitted to one puppet because you only have two hands with which to control them. Decide which parts will move and use split pins to act as joints. Attach the rods so that the moving parts can be controlled, like the dinosaur below.

The Shadow Theatre
Position your theatre so that a strong light shines through from the back. A powerful torch is a good light source. There must be room for the puppeteer to crouch below the screen or to stand at the side clear of the path of the light. If the puppeteer stands below the screen, then you will need to cover the space below with a curtain. If he or she stands in the wings, use screens or hang curtains at the sides.

The Performance
Sort out the characters before the performance placing them on the correct side of the screen. Stand them upright in plastic containers until they are needed. Arrange them in the correct order of appearance. Carry out rehearsals in front of a mirror to see how your play looks from the audience. Do you need any shadow scenery? It could be slotted into place. Think about sound effects, music or dialogue.

Dinosaur Shadow Puppets

Puppets with Strings

Puppets are made all over the world so there are many different ideas to consider. A shadow puppet is a rigid, two-dimensional shape. A marionette, or stringed puppet, is a flexible, three-dimensional figure. For centuries, puppet shows have told well-known legends and folk tales The size of a puppet determines the way it moves. In India, a one-stringed puppet is traditional. In Japan, the huge Bunraku puppet needs three operators.

Designing a Marionette
Choose materials that are light but strong. A heavy puppet will be difficult to control. Look at the example shown here. The basic body structure has been shaped from twisted pipe cleaners. To make 'joints', loops have been made at the end of the pipe cleaners. It is important that these joints move very freely.

For hands and feet use large, heavy buttons. They can be attached easily to the pipe cleaners and the operating strings can also be threaded through them.

For the head use a ball of sponge or pressed cotton. A pipe cleaner 'neck' can be pushed into the head and secured with glue.

Strings
Use strong string that will withstand lots of pulling. To begin with, keep the stringing simple. The head and all four limbs will need separate strings. Measure each string carefully to ensure that the lengths are in proportion, then attach them to a control bar like the one below.

Movement in Puppets
You can achieve a greater degree of movement by attaching strings to the knee and elbow joints as well. As you gain experience as a puppeteer, you will be able to control more complex characters that need many more strings.

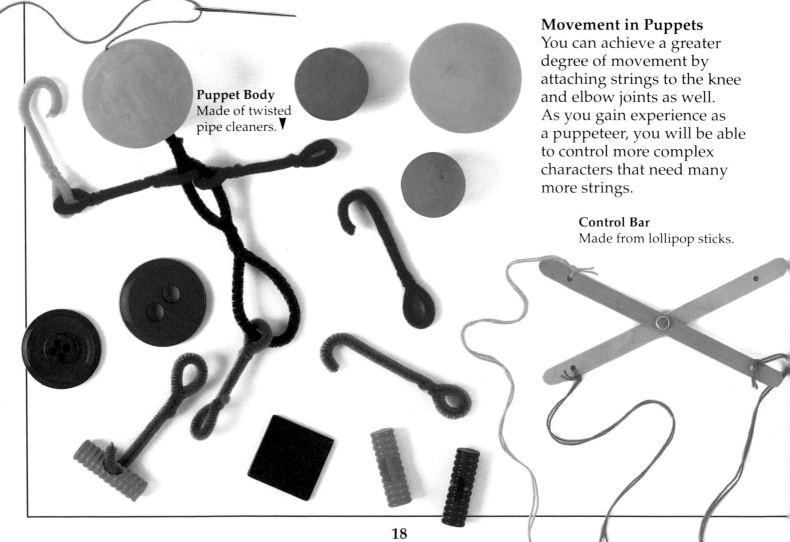

Puppet Body
Made of twisted pipe cleaners. ▼

Control Bar
Made from lollipop sticks.

Movement in People

The human skeleton contains over 200 bones. It is an efficient system of joints and levers that allow the body to move freely. Where two bones meet, they form a joint. The body has many different joints and each works with the help of muscles fixed to the bones by tendons.

Features and Costumes

Once the basic puppet figure is made, you can turn it into any character that you wish. Cut and glue felt features on to the face. Use fabric for the costume and either sew or glue the pieces together. Make sure that the clothing is loose and baggy so that the puppet's movements are not hindered in any way.

Storing a Marionette

After any rehearsal or performance, the puppets must be stored away safely otherwise, if they become damaged, all the hard work put into their construction will be wasted. Can you design a means of storage that will prevent the strings from becoming entangled?

Puppet Theatres

The puppet theatre is the focus of attention for both the audience in front and the puppeteers behind. It is the centre of much bustling activity before, during and after each performance. For these reasons you need a rigid and **stable** structure. If you are taking the trouble to make a puppet theatre, you will expect to use it many times and you will want it to be sturdy. Fixing additional supports to the outside adds extra stability.

Building a Theatre
Before you begin to construct, first sketch out your ideas and plan the whole design. You will need a strong, open-topped box large enough to contain your puppets comfortably. Measure and cut away the front and sides of the box as shown below. Score and fold back the sides to make hinged flaps. These flaps will also provide support. Along the top of each 'wing' measure and cut parallel notches.

Scenery
Scenery flats, back cloth and curtain can all be attached to rods held in place in parallel notches. Design and paint the back cloth and scenery flats on stiff card. Use bright colours that will be seen from the back of the audience. Each piece of scenery must hang vertically, without curling up at the edges. Attach each piece to a rod with tape as shown.

Curtains
The stage curtain will be raised and lowered frequently between scenes. Use a piece of crease-resistant fabric that does not fray and is slightly wider than the front opening. Glue or tape one end of the fabric to a rod and roll up the rest. Place the rolled curtain in the parallel notches nearest to the front of the stage. You can have a variety of scenery changes and curtains for different performances.

Constructing a Puppet Theatre

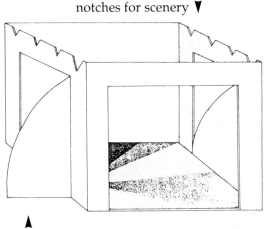

notches for scenery ▼

▲
Cut out side and front openings from a box.

curtain on roller ▼   scenery flats and backdrop rods ►

Decorating the Theatre

A puppet theatre must also look attractive. The audience will be watching your puppeteering skills and will gain added pleasure if you have spent time decorating your theatre. The theatre below can be used both for marionettes and puppets with side rods—the marionettes lowered from above, the rod puppets controlled from the side.

Lighting

To create effective stage lighting position small torches covered with coloured tissue paper in the wings behind the hinged flap.

Alternatively, use batteries with small bulbs connected in series in an electrical circuit. Position the bulbs, like footlights, at the front of the stage and conceal the batteries in the wings.

Staging a Performance

You will have decided by now upon the story line for your performance but do you need extra sound effects or music? These could be pre-recorded on tape. When all the rehearsals are over and you are satisfied with the show, you are ready to invite the audience. Design a special programme and advertise with posters.Try to make the performance as professional as possible.

Puppet Theatre

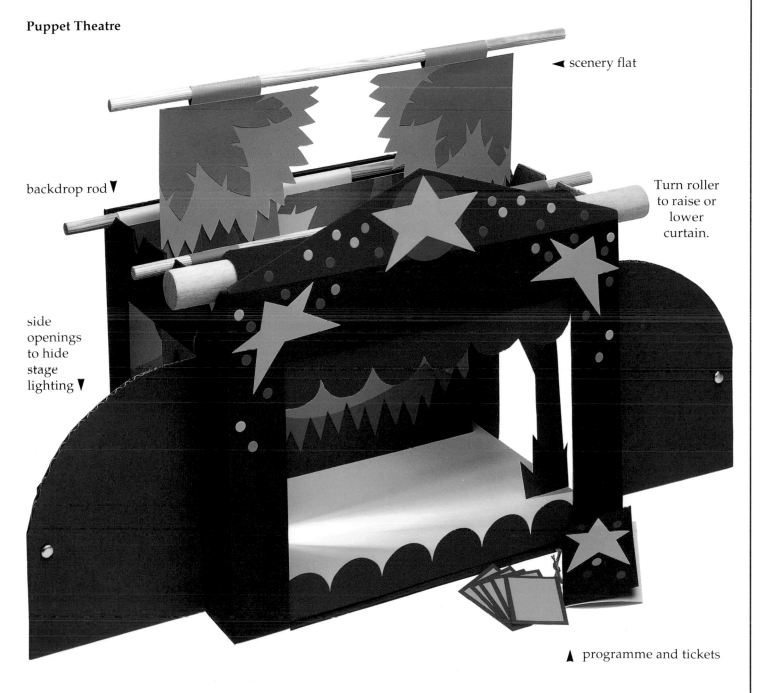

◄ scenery flat

backdrop rod ▼

Turn roller to raise or lower curtain.

side openings to hide stage lighting ▼

▲ programme and tickets

Jumping Jacks

Some toys have levers to make them work. A lever is a bar that rotates around a point known as a pivot or fulcrum. Your forearm is a lever, your elbow is the pivot. The effect of a lever is to increase a force allowing a small amount of energy, a pull or a push, to produce a large movement. Levers joined together to form a linkage produce a number of movements at the same time. This is how a jumping jack works.

Linkages

A linkage is built by joining a series of levers together. It can change the direction and the distance at which the levers work. Very little effort is needed to create a dramatic movement. Look around you and see how series of levers and linkages are used in everyday life to aid movement.

Making a Linkage

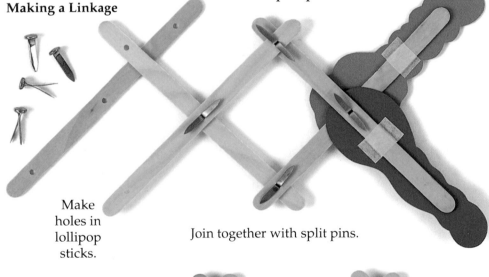

Make holes in lollipop sticks.

Snapping Crocodile

The snapping crocodile works when slight pressure is placed on the two 'handles' squeezing them together. The resulting movement causes the whole series of joints along the length of the crocodile to close, including the crocodile's mouth. Open the handles and the mouth snaps open.

Join together with split pins.

Constructing a Linkage

Use lollipop sticks to make a network linked together with split pins as shown below. The sticks should extend and retract in a scissor movement.

Make a face for the crocodile out of stiff card. Attach the upper part of the face and jaw to the top stick and the lower part to the bottom. Pivot the face at the centre with a split pin which is also pushed through the sticks.

Design a similar toy that has a vertical action rather than a horizontal one, like a frog hopping up and down.

Attach face parts to sticks with tape.

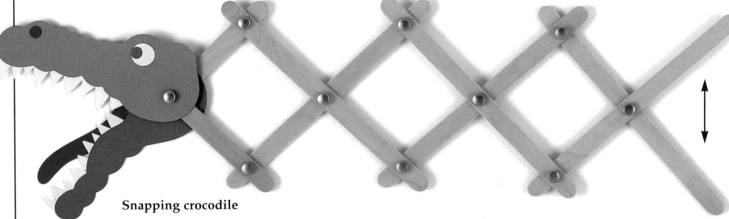

Snapping crocodile

Jumping Jacks

A jumping jack is a two-dimensional, jointed figure made from wood or card. It makes a single jerky movement when a string is pulled.
With a marionette, each string causes a separate movement.

The movement produced by a lever depends on the position of the pivot.
A jumping jack, like the snapping crocodile, is a linkage—a series of joints or levers. Its pivot points are where the split pins join the limbs to the body.

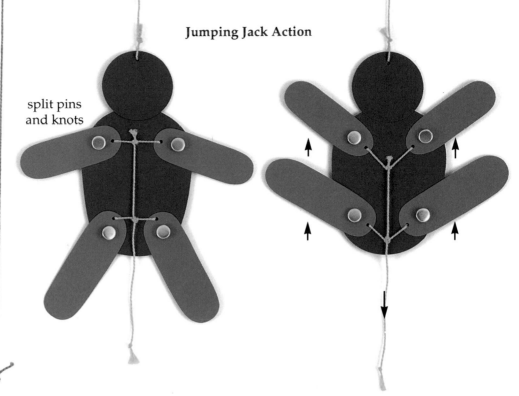

split pins and knots

Jumping Jack Action

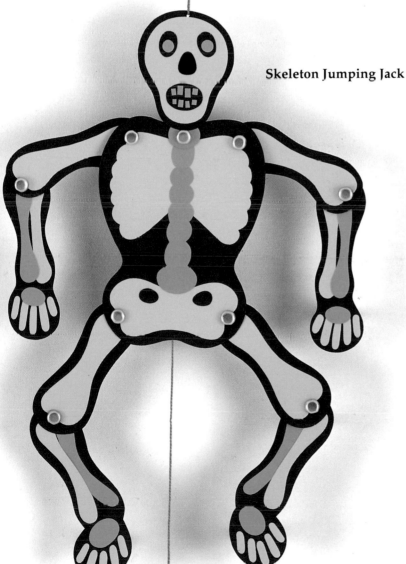

Skeleton Jumping Jack

Dancing Skeleton

Design a skeleton jumping jack. How many bones can you move with one pull? Draw the shape on card and cut out the body and limbs separately. Follow the diagram above to join the parts together with split pins. Connect the limbs as shown here with strong thread.

To make your figure work, suspend it so it hangs freely and pull the thread. Watch it jump! Think of designing a character where different parts of the body move, like a nodding head or wagging tail.

Try making freely suspended joints at the knees and elbows as well. They will kick out wildly when the central thread is pulled. Very little energy is needed to do a lot of work.

Wheeled Toys

If you try to push a heavy load along the ground, it will be very hard work because of the weight of the load and a force called **friction**. Friction occurs when two objects rub together. Reducing friction makes things move more easily. Centuries ago, people discovered that heavy loads were easier to move on rollers. Later, they invented wheels with axles. Wheels reduce friction and make heavy loads easier to move.

Simple Wheeled Toys

Movement in simple wheeled toys is achieved by pushing or pulling. Simple wheeled toys can be made from junk materials. Collect four identical lids and make a hole in the centre of each. Attach the lids to cartons and boxes using split pins. Make a road train, like those used in Australia, by joining together several wheeled boxes to pull along.

Try pushing your vehicle uphill. Which is easier, pulling or pushing?

Wheels and Axles

The wheeled trucks shown here do not have axles, so the materials to make them must be as light as possible to reduce the load, keeping friction to a minimum. By joining opposite wheels with an axle, friction is reduced even further, so heavier materials can be used to make the vehicle. Try designing a wheeled toy with axles.

Eccentric Wheels

When the wheels of a toy are positioned off-centre, it becomes an eccentric wheeled toy. To achieve the right effect, one wheel must be 'up' when the other is 'down'. The toy should have a rocking motion as it is pulled along.

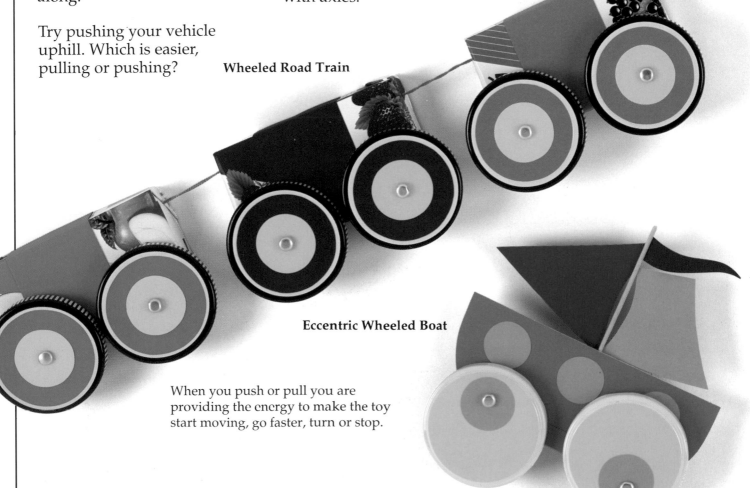

Wheeled Road Train

Eccentric Wheeled Boat

When you push or pull you are providing the energy to make the toy start moving, go faster, turn or stop.

A Flapping Butterfly

Make an axle by attaching two lids to a length of dowel with small nails. Make a slit in a cork, as shown below, and attach it to the axle with a piece of card. Copy the butterfly pattern on to thin card and decorate it creasing along the folds. Slot the butterfly into the cork and glue it into place.

Make holes in the card butterfly, as indicated, and pierce a hole near the rim of each wheel. Line up the wheels so the holes are level. Thread stiff wire through the hole in the wheel to the butterfly wing above and repeat on the other side.

Attach a length of rod as a handle to the butterfly by glueing it firmly to the cork. When the butterfly is pushed along its wings will flap. Fix small bells to the wings. These will ring as it flies along.

Wheels in Action

We have used lids for wheels. It is very important that they are all the same diameter. Which works best plastic or metal? The more shiny they are, the less friction there is. If you push your vehicle down a slippery slope how can you control its speed? Try positioning rubber bands around the lid rims. This will increase friction and prevent slipping like the thick tread on lorry tyres.

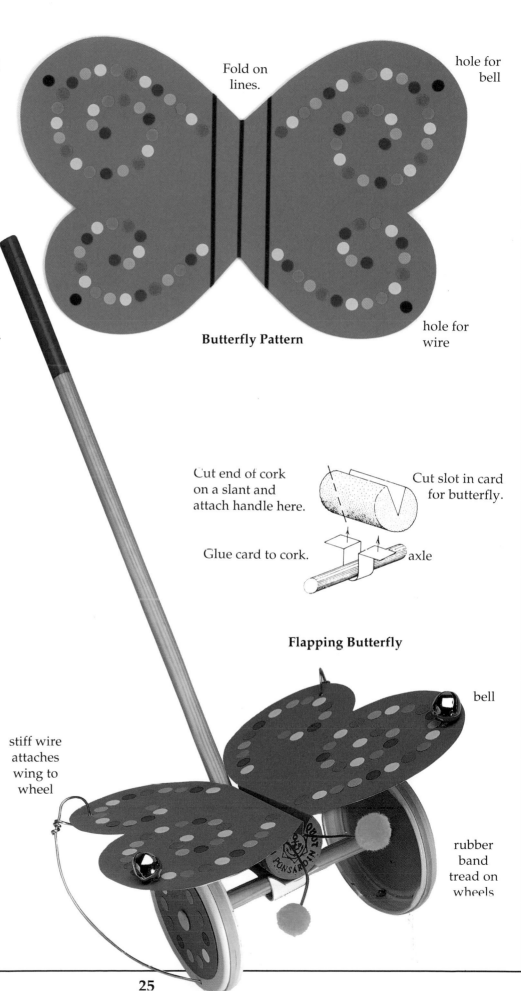

Fold on lines.

hole for bell

hole for wire

Butterfly Pattern

Cut end of cork on a slant and attach handle here.

Cut slot in card for butterfly.

Glue card to cork.

axle

Flapping Butterfly

stiff wire attaches wing to wheel

bell

rubber band tread on wheels

Spring Toys

Springs were first used in clocks about 400 years ago. The spring was wound up each day and then as it slowly unwound, it turned the hands. A similar mechanism is sometimes used in toys. If you have a clockwork toy, wind it up and watch what happens to the spring as the toy moves. Energy is stored in the spring as it is wound up. As it unwinds, the stored energy changes to energy of movement.

Jumping Bugs

To make a jumping bug, you need a rubber suction pad, a round card base, smaller in diameter than the suction pad, a length of stiff wire and a 'bug'. Push one end of the spring into the suction pad and glue the bug to it. Tape the other end of the spring to the card base. It is important that the sharp ends of the spring are protected. Attach the card base to a flat surface, press the bug down and watch it spring up.

Springs

Metal springs are used in many everyday objects such as chairs, cars and mattresses. A spring has **elasticity** because of its shape.

A **compressed** spring stores energy. Releasing the spring allows the energy to become movement, or kinetic, energy.

Try using other materials to make a jumping toy like elastic bands or sponge.

Movement

Every time stored energy is released and changes into kinetic energy, something moves. Think about ways of using an elastic band to store and release energy. Why does a catapult work? (If you make one be very careful. Only aim at safe targets.)

Try making a musical instrument that relies on a vibrating string to make sound.

Jumping Bugs

Make bugs from woolly pom-poms or sponge balls. Add eyes and wobbling antennae.

suction pads

A Scurrying Spider

To make a motor for a scurrying spider, first find a flexible, plastic lid. Make three holes in the lid in the positions shown. Bend wire across the lid, fixing it through the two opposite holes and taping it into place.

Divide the hole at the centre of a cotton reel into two halves with a piece of card. Thread elastic through the reel, attaching it around the wire. Secure a length of string to the cotton reel and then wind it round the reel.
Pass the other end through the remaining hole in the lid.

Decorate your spider giving it pipe cleaner legs, a head and antennae.

Hold the spider on the floor and pull the string. Then let go and watch it scurry across the floor.

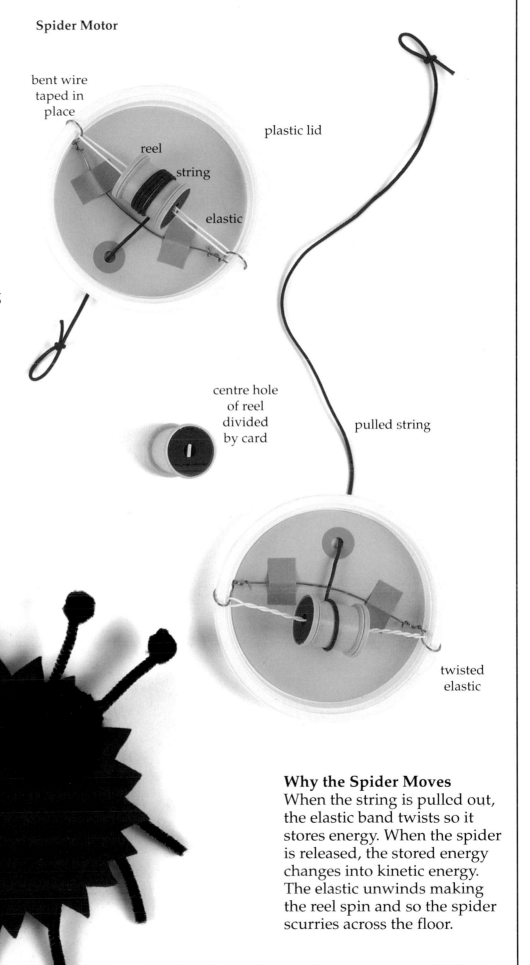

Spider Motor

bent wire taped in place

plastic lid

reel

string

elastic

centre hole of reel divided by card

pulled string

twisted elastic

Scurrying Spider

Why the Spider Moves

When the string is pulled out, the elastic band twists so it stores energy. When the spider is released, the stored energy changes into kinetic energy. The elastic unwinds making the reel spin and so the spider scurries across the floor.

Cogs and Wheels

Not all wheels move along when they turn, some stay in the same place. They have teeth known as cogs cut into their rims. The cogs of one wheel fit into the cogs of the next wheel. If the first wheel turns so does the next one. If the cog wheels are different sizes, they turn at different speeds. Cog wheels are called gears. Gears are used in toys to transmit movement from one part of the toy to another.

Turning Cog Wheels

The speed at which cog wheels turn depends on how many teeth they have. If one wheel has 30 teeth and another has 15 teeth, then when the larger wheel turns once, the smaller wheel must turn twice. It must also turn twice as fast. Cog wheels change the direction of movement because each one turns the next one in the opposite direction.

Fortune Wheels

Design a set of fortune wheels like the ones shown below. First make a pair of cog wheels, one twice the **circumference** of the other with twice as many teeth. Position them on a card base with their teeth meshing. Secure them both through their centres using split pins making sure that they turn freely. Make a flap in the larger wheel that can be lifted up.

Glue a small handle to the small wheel. When the handle is turned, both wheels revolve. Stop the wheels and life the flap. A message or fortune written underneath will be revealed.

Design a game with several cog wheels of different sizes. How many can you make turn at once? Notice that the smallest wheel turns fastest.

Fortune Wheels

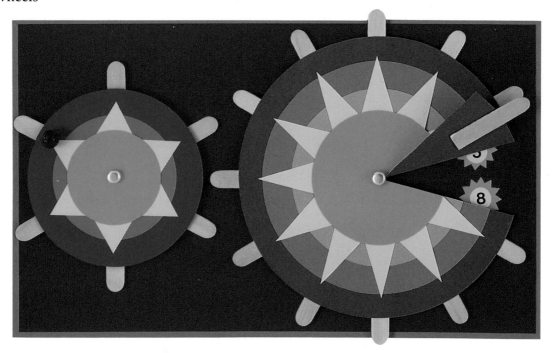

Make the cog wheels by cutting up lollipop sticks and glueing the pieces around a card circle. Cut an opening flap in the large wheel.

Write a number of scores or messages on the card base under the large wheel. When the flap is lifted, one of the messages will be seen.

Space Roundabout

Movement in the space roundabout is transmitted by cog wheels but they are arranged at 90° so that the smaller wheel is vertical and the larger wheel is horizontal.

Make two cogs, one large and one small, and position them at 90° to one another on a box. Secure them with split pins through their centres. Make sure the teeth mesh together and that the wheels turn freely. The horizontal cog wheel could be mounted on to a circular box lid.

Make a space roundabout with space ships and planets made from plastic junk materials or modelling clay. The models must not be too heavy. Arrange them on to a piece of dowel and glue the dowel to the centre of the horizontal cog as shown here.

Centrifugal Force

When the handle on the small cog is turned, the roundabout moves. If some parts of the space models are not rigidly attached, the spinning movement will cause them to lift up and fly through the air.

Centrifugal force pulls the models away from the rotating central axis. The faster the axis turns the greater the force, pulling the models almost horizontal.

Make sure all the models are very firmly attached before the roundabout is rotated.

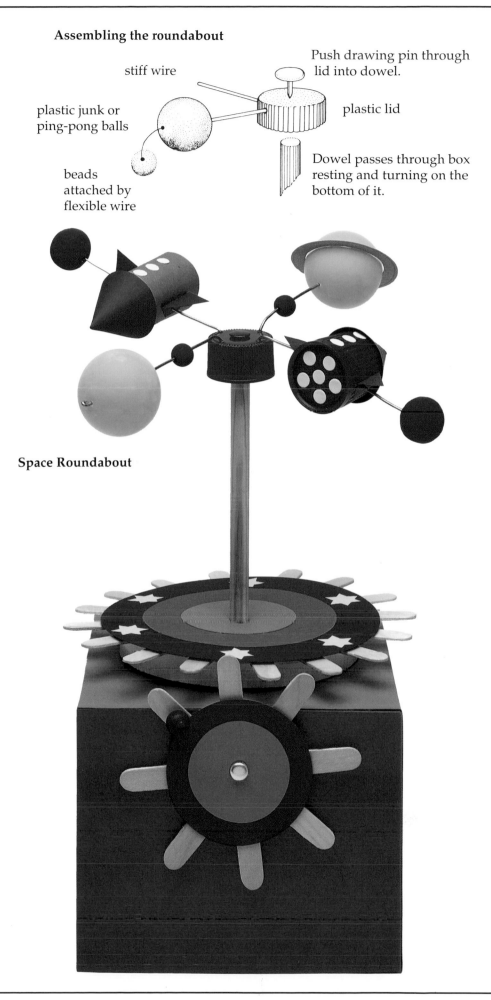

Assembling the roundabout

stiff wire

plastic junk or ping-pong balls

Push drawing pin through lid into dowel.

plastic lid

beads attached by flexible wire

Dowel passes through box resting and turning on the bottom of it.

Space Roundabout

Kites and Windmills

Some toys use natural sources of energy to make them move. Kites and windmills move by wind energy. A kite can be three-dimensional or two-dimensional. It should be light but strong and flexible. The Chinese regard kite-flying as an art form. Their first kites were made from whatever natural materials were available—often bamboo covered with silk or paper. Kites and windmills are toys but they also have important working uses for people.

Single and Double Windmills
To make a single windmill, cut a square from thin paper. Cut slits as in diagram *A*. Fold and pin all the points into the centre.

For the double windmill cut out both squares *A* and *B*, and fit them together as in *C*. Fit the windmill on to a stick with a pin threading a small bead between the stick and the windmill. This will allow it to turn freely.

Place both windmills in a windy spot and watch them turn. Do you expect the double windmill to turn faster than the single one?

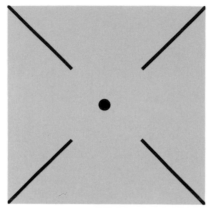

A Single Windmill

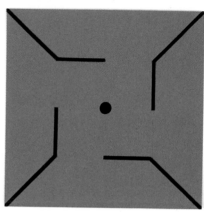

B Double Windmill

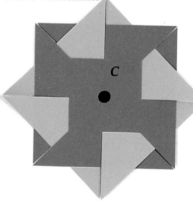

C

Place a bead between the windmill and the stick.

Use a glass headed pin to attach the windmill to the stick.

A Diamond Kite

This is a classic kite design. All the materials needed to make it must be light and strong. Cut a diamond shape from coloured polythene or plastic. Tape triangular sections to each corner to strengthen them. They need to be strong to hold the frame of the kite. Cut two light wooden sticks to fit the kite and bind them together at the point where they cross in the centre.

Cut tails and tassels from plastic strips and attach them to the tail and the corners. These can be adjusted to improve the stability if necessary. Attach the flying line to the tail and centre point.

Tape triangular sections to each corner to attach frame.

light wooden sticks for frame

Tassels and tails help stability and control when flying.

Flying your Kite

A force called lift makes the kite rise as the wind moves past it. Ask someone to hold your kite facing into the wind. You must run into the wind when they let go. Play out the string to make the kite fly higher.

Never fly your kite near overhead cables. Choose somewhere with few trees and no buildings.

Word List

centrifugal force A force acting outward from the centre of a rotating object.

circumference The distance around the edge of a circle.

compressed Forced into less space. Squeezed together.

diagonal A straight line joining two corners of a polygon that are not adjacent.

durable Lasting for a long time.

eccentric Positioned off centre.

elasticity The ability of a material to return to its original shape after compression or stretching.

flexible Materials that can be bent easily without breaking.

friction The force created when two materials rub against each other. Friction opposes movement. No movement means no friction.

function The intended purpose of something. The theory of design, or functionalism, states that the form of a thing should be decided by its use.

hexagon A six-sided polygon.

horizontal In a position parallel to the horizon.

magnetic forces Invisible forces causing attraction or repulsion between magnetic materials.

octagon An eight-sided polygon.

opaque Not allowing light to pass through.

parallel Two or more lines lying side by side an equal distance apart at every point.

polygonal An adjective describing a closed, plane figure having three or more straight sides.

portable Able to be carried by hand.

rigid Stiff or inflexible, not easy to bend.

stable Balanced, not easily moved.

strategy A special plan devised to ensure success in a game.

structure Parts joined together to make a whole

synthetic materials Materials made by people. Raw materials chemically changed into another substance.

tactile Relating to the sense of touch.

translucent Allowing some light to pass through.

vertical Upright, at right angles to the horizon.

vertices Plural of vertex. The points where two edges meet on a solid shape like a pyramid.

Index